Ghost in the Window

"we are getting a mist, the kind ghosts navigate in..."

Donna Allard

International Beat Poet Laureate

Heartfelt thanks to

the community of Kent County, New Brunswick

Ronda Wicks Eller, Brian Stevens

and the National Beat Poet Foundation Inc., CT, US

for their support and encouragement.

Ghost in the Window

Author: Donna Allard (1956-)

Cover photo credit: Donna Allard
Editor: Ronda Wicks Eller
Photo credits: Claude Vautour, Donna Allard

Indexed.

ISBN 978-0-9738671-9-0
First Edition, 2019

Publisher:
River Bones Press
New Brunswick, Canada

river
bones
press
New Brunswick,
Canada

riverbonespress.wixsite.com/rbpress

Editor's Foreword

In this personal collection Donna Allard provides her readers with a snapshot of her years growing up, time missed with parents while away at high school during her mother's battle with cancer and the continuing love that both demonstrated during moments of reprieve. There is a sense of the everlastingness that comes from moments when her memories flood in and then abate repeatedly. She doesn't shy away from addressing the awkwardness of youth or the feeling of sometimes being talked about and watched, perhaps judged, by people who have no business doing so.

The entire collection can be read as a chain-work of thought as life progresses and is presented in an interesting mixture of poems and prose that read much like a journal.

As the editor, I found this book a joy to read and work through, very nearly coming to tears of my own at one point where I not only related but experienced a certain depth of the despair Donna must have felt at that point in her life. It's a very intimate offering!

~ Ronda Wicks Eller

Ghost in the Window

"we are getting a mist, the kind ghosts navigate in"

Poems Index

Introduction

The year was 2010, down an old dirt road sat a little old weather beaten house, owned by two elderly ladies that passed away some years before. It was a small house built back in the early 1900s from a lumber-baron's mill, as the story was told to me by his granddaughter. The house stood alone in a field with over grown bushes and 100 year old trees.

The white 'for sale' sign was in the ditch near the end of the lane. The tip of the corner peered out from between tall grass blades. When I got home I called to ask if it was still for sale; the answer was YES.

The following Sunday I took photos of the house, remembering a dream: an old house in the middle of a field, bothered by no one.

I took many pictures that day - the sun was warm and sky was blue, but I never bothered to look at the photos that evening -- dreams were blossoming.

Later that week I called again, to ask what the selling price was, saddened to learn that it was out of my range. I never gave it another thought until one day the owners called and said, "Can you come over? We have something to tell you," and off I went. They said they had many offers on the place but wanted it to go to a good family. What outlined how, back in the day when my father was a the town physician, he made housecalls to give the elderly sharp-witted women (the owners' aunts) health check-ups and pick up homemade bread, pies and daffodil bouquets.

Their niece gave me the key to look inside and there, sitting by the old wood stove, was the rocking chair my dad sat in when he stopped by.

With camera in hand I snapped photos left and right, and then it was time to go. After closing the door I took a final snapshot of the entrance porch and when I arrived at my apartment I placed the chip in the computer slot to upload the files.

Late that night, after looking them over and showing them to friends online, someone said, "Do you see what is in the window?

Look closely, you will see the ghost waving, as if it was saying thank you, the house is yours."

Ghost
dedicated to the one in our 1909 farm

i see the ghost in the far window
observing something.
click click

—

focus focus

—

thought flash

—

these kind eyes
obviously
unaware. introspective. Quietude.

It Was July 31st, 1970s

car packed
groceries in trunk
trunk lid shut hard-cocked
doors slammed...
My parents and I drove west
from the fishing village of Richibucto
to arrive south in the city of Fredericton.

My apartment was on a hill so
spring flooding behind Fredericton High School
would never affect me.

Mom filled the kitchen cupboards,
toilet necessities and Kotex were
stored in the bathroom,
boxes in the living room,
suitcases piled on the pull-out bed.
It was a damp basement dwelling.

They kidnapped me like pirates
and took me to unknown lands.
I watched them leave through flooded wasteland,
my mind awash in thoughts that swam
downstream on waves of memory –
ones that relentlessly overtook them
until they drowned.

Well, It's August 1st

I decide to do a walk-about
headed west, then south,
the fragrant aromas of fresh
baked breads, cakes and donuts
awoke my hunger as I entered
Dominion Grocery.

Dad and I used to stop at Dominion
in Moncton every week. I loved seeing
his childlike eyes widen into big,
full moons.

But this time my stop was moonless –
being alone.

Labor Day Weekend

Another walk-about
down the hills to main street:
I should have had a skateboard.
I was met by a black cat sleeping
on the corner of Brunswick and York,
the only spot of sunlight between the tall
buildings. the only car out was a taxi
that went around her; the driver
must have been a cat lover.

1st Day Fredericton High

Gee, so many students
scurrying around and round like mice
a maze of staircases and doors and
a registration desk - what the f** is that?
after all the t's and i's were crossed and dotted
I left with homework.

Day 2

Factory day at Fredericton High:
less mice around but one rat –
me, looking for an easy way out.
I sat in the cafeteria all day,
then walked to Micky D's
with no homework.

Day 3

No phone call from mom or dad
in over a month. I found out later
that mom was in Saint John Hospital
getting cancer treatments.
I never told them I knew.

Thanksgiving

I arrived in Richibucto by bus
walked home to find it empty
and locked. After interviewing
all the neighbors I walked
to the cottage 3 miles south
and ate canned beans & crackers
left from summer.

Christmas Holiday

After another bus ride from hell
and drunk old men grabbing me at
every opportunity (why I never
ride a bus as first choice)

I found mom at the kitchen sink,
dad working in the office.
Mom never even looked back when I said
"I'm Home!' smiling from ear to ear.

December 25th

Opening gifts. Bacon and eggs brekky. Mom smiling at
the beautiful Christmas tree. She had every right to - it
was gorgeous (like every Christmas before). She *loved*
this season and it showed, but one thing missing was
turkey dinner, wine and deserts. Then the doorbell rang.
Friends from Aldouane had arrived bearing gifts of a 24
lb turkey with *all* the fixin's (even deserts, poutins). No
wine-sparkling except for that of glowing hearth-warmed
hearts.

New Years Eve

Watched events on TV.

New Years Day

Getting ready to leave for Fredericton:
dad was driving me, it felt like old times.
We laughed. I talked about the new school
and how the teachers wanted me to take
top-level classes but I refused, wondering
how a girl from Richibucto could be that smart.
He stopped at Dominion, and
his full moons appeared. After a kiss
and hug he left for home, leaving me
to walk to my apartment feeling homeless
and flooded again.
I ate the donut weeping,
not because I missed him or mom
but because the universe
could never be the same again,
not even with Dominion's aromas
lingering down my street.

Valentines

I gave myself a card
and postage stamped mom & dads.
Theirs was returned—
cancer has a way of distorting reality.

Feb 25 Birthday

Didn't get a call. The postman carried a box: my parents'
gift filled with snacks, clothing and books – everything I
loved, with a card/letter saying they looked forward to
seeing me at Easter, that I better fast, and ending it with
"We Love YOU!, in classical doctors handwriting

Easter

I began by looking behind furniture,
under linen-draped tables, under chairs,
inside the fireplace, upstairs under beds
and in closets, in mom's makeup table jars
and *I Found Them!*
The Cadbury eggs were
in each of my parents' hands
enough smiles on their faces
to melt them too.

Last Day of School

Dad bought me a car –
one that drunk hands
would never be permitted to touch.
It was my first real road trip.
I was free!

Summer

I sat through most of it with mom in the sunroom
as she teased me about fryin' up the *huge*
goldfish in the aquarium. I always believed she would.

She spent every afternoon talking to me as I laid on the
couch. She told me family stories about her past as a
teen, how she met dad... spaghetti (but I'll leave that for
another book, wink).

She was a very strong woman with a dry wit, clever as a
fox, loving and kind and a great cook. It was difficult
to see her in her favorite chair– she used to tower over it
at 5' 10" but now she sat like a child awaiting an abusive
Father.

That is what cancer is...

July

Dad couldn't go to the funeral, advised against it by his Doctor, for fear of a heart attack. I sat at home with him. Everyone hated me after that, and dad too. They never took the time to ask why and still don't. Dad put the house up for sale and I returned to Fredericton to find my place flooded, so I returned home again.

* My uncle Ernest, dad's brother, died at the funeral of his wife. My cousins buried both parents a week later. Dad didn't want this for his daughters.

Photo credit: Claude Vautour

Cottage Life On Richibucto River

Asleep and secure, I'm awakened by footsteps.
My dog is also awake and marching about. This assures
me that I am not hearing things; judging by his stance
there is someone on the roof, and it's not Santa.

I reach for warmer clothing, boots and gun (unloaded).
Together we walk about, quietly listening, and there it is
again, and then gone.
I begin to breathe a little easier.

At 6:30 am, I phone dad. He says he will be here shortly
and his trust in me is encouraging. I open the door to
take a look outside for footprints but nothing is visible on
the moonlit fresh-fallen snow.

My father has to park the car up the road and walk
down, so we met and go inside where I explain
everything. He goes outside and walks around, nothing is
disturbed beyond the scope of our own foot prints. We
conclude that it may have been guys trying to scare me
(they are like that around here) but they must have been
pretty ingenious to leave no tracks. Dad stayed for
breakfast and later went to his office. Could it have been
a bobcat or lynx? Could it have been a ghost?

I'll never know – but the fear never left me.

Walking On Water

Dad was closing up the cottage for the season and I handed logs to him, to chop for the last time. We loved hearing the crackling of birch while sipping hot cider on cold summer evenings. Once when I was 8 I took a long walk along the shoreline and each step cracked like a branch with a crisp clear echo. All bundled up, I ran with arms outward like a plane while dad boarded the windows and drained the water pipes for the long cold winter. I ran with eyes closed, the winter sun warming my face. I ran and I ran.

I walked on water!

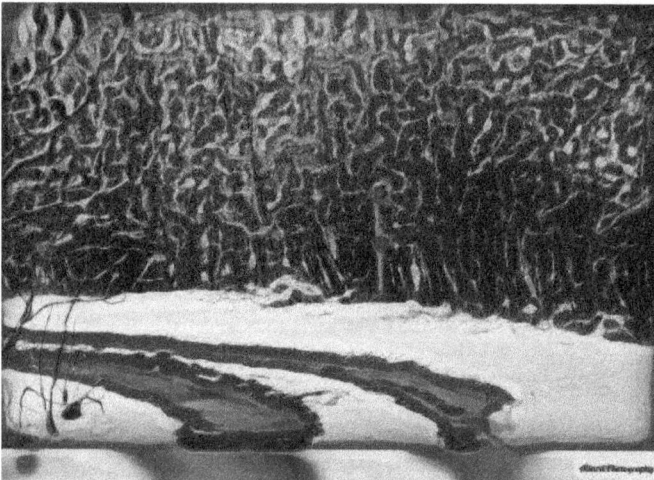

Have We Met Before

dedicated to poet Colin Haskins
vacations to Maine

Have we met? I am sure we did as children
strolling at Old Orchard Beach,
as tides faded lovers' footprints
far into the copper sunset sands,

when at the Bucksport Cemetery
I hear my relatives' bones rattle
in anticipation of my arrival and feel you
as falling leaves before my feet.

There was a time in a Portland restaurant
I swear your laugh was a short distance away.
Glancing behind the counter as morning rays glowed
in the mirror reflecting a smile - mine

warming as sun-rays on a cold winters' dusk.
Later that evening like a raven questing over deep
blue seas, search for a kindred spirit.

Dory

Unless I go to NFLD it's nearly impossible to find an old Dory beached like a whale, unless you know of a hidden spot where old dories go to rest.

On these Acadian shores beer cans rest, old charcoal remnants of a late night party, a missing Nike. I can't figure out how one forgets their footwear let alone a cooler, but I've found both and more on my footpath.

Recently, while poking around coves along the Maine coast, I found a faded brick red Dory majestically posing in sparkling blue waters. It was a lost photo opportunity.

One summer I asked my father to buy me a boat and a week later it was waiting along the shore at our cottage in Rexton. It wore the appearance of a previously life-weathered and gruff old salt. I heard the vaguely curtained giggles of neighbors as I pushed it into the river.

The old dory shoved off eagerly and I boarded her. Her hearty oars kissed and cavorted with the waves as we headed to the island. Every cottager laughed at me and my Dory - a 10 year old sailing the high seas.

I even wore a sea captain's hat!

Note: NFLD – province of Newfoundland & Labrador; my mother was born in Cornerbrook, NFLD.

Leonard Cohen

My teen years were teased out with poetry by
Leonard Cohen awakening my sensuality. His words
penetrated and his seed found a home for what
seemed an eternity, and then a breaking of blood-
stained waters shed the fruit– a rebirth as this shaky
hand picked up a pen and breathed life through this
body's smooth parchment. Stained in indigo and
autographed
All my love,
Donna

Tempest In A Teapot

The morning sun reflects on the day's events
as the newspaper lays silent on this old table,
its butternut pine hue warming the room,
my Padermo teapot awakens the household.
This is a good morning to sit outside
and read this new book by Nino Ricci
my tea at hand and all being right with the world.

Last Sunday is another world away now,
a stream of events slowly drifting from memory
but a gentle reminder that all is not always
right with the world. Will this Sunday begin
like a tempest in my teapot? An unforgiving
storm of words written in anger
without the slightest gesture to be kind?
An over inked pen spoiling the sanctity of the day?

The evening is setting as warm as
children's morning laughter from a window.
It brings a mother's smile to my motherless face.
How lucky I am to bear witness to these little joys
that life gives us so freely - a book
interesting enough to warrant a lamp,
cold tea by my side, and laughter
to complete the day.

Kouchibouguac Squatter

inspired by Metis activist Jackie Vautour

Salt cod breath, wood-chipping lumber jacket,
bright orange hunting vest, toque over ears,
eye of the sun resting on the shoulders of
Jackie Vautour as the fight to survive continues,
his roots firmly planted - a maple surrounded by
pine and spruce.

The fall's last salty breeze freezing
on the CBC's cold video cameras,
the mic recording the voice of the land,
media trucks and cars lining the highway at
Kouchibouguac like a marriage procession
at a shotgun wedding.

Dangerous Shoal

the mightiest winds
the greatest of seas
abandoned edges
  of what life could be

Riverbanks

dedicated to the fisher people of Kent County N.B.

Along riverbanks, old memories
wrapped in cigarette papers
dangle like a fish hook,
thin pale pages of history
read like a map –
here-a-bouts ramshackle
fishing shacks cast blood
into the mouth of this river,
gutted fish tales that never
reach shore.

Vein Memories

inspired by poet Anis Mojgani

Blank eyes. blank page.
    blank. blank. blank.
My vein memories
in red. in blue.
        in you.
    I transfix myself
screaming behind your eyes –
a ghost held
    in vein bondage
releasing sweet Sunday kisses.
Shake Him. Shake yourself.
    Shake.
Alive this midnight god of insanity.

My vein universality
is freed by a cup of Love
upheld by an imperceptible
      cloudy hand.

The Ghost Who Is Now Me

Tribute to Canada's Peoples' Poet Milton Acorn, PEI

There was a man named Acorn
who was adored by many a few,
now outcasted by a tittered latent Isle;
an indigo literary vision of old' Charlottetown's
Victorian Row. I was young, too young
to know why a man chose a life so wretched
in most people's eyes.

Cornered once during a walk looked me eye to eye,
but I still couldn't see this thirst for knowledge he
wished to share
but thankfully people unlike me
saw within those eyes --
let it not be forgotten:
a certain Acorn fell from a Red Oak Tree and, picking
it up from its earthy base, a privileged wisdom many
will never see was passed along.

An indigo Raven weeps a silent tear's journey, etches
a rainbow in the silken blue Island skies.

Thank you!
I hope you enjoyed
this poetic journal

Love to you all,

Donna Allard

river bones press
poems & stuff
New Brunswick,
Canada

Official River Bones Website:
https://riverbonespress.wixsite.com/rbpress

Photo credit: Donna Allard
Richibucto Riverbanks & Dory

www.ingramcontent.com/pod-product-compliance
Lightning Source LLC
Chambersburg PA
CBHW022351040426
42449CB00006B/820